LAST
POETIC GEMS

William McGonagall

Poet and Tragedian

Died in Edinburgh 29th September, 1902

DUCKWORTH

First published in this edition 1980

Gerald Duckworth & Co Ltd
The Old Piano Factory
43 Gloucester Crescent, London NW1

ISBN 0 7156 0613 1

Typeset by Elanders Computer Assisted
Typesetting Systems, Inverness
and printed and bound in Great Britain by
Redwood Burn Limited
Trowbridge and Esher

CONTENTS

Farewell Address at the Argyle Hall...................... 7
The Last Berkshire Eleven: the Heroes of Maiwand.......... 8
The Demon Drink..................................... 12
Grif, of the Bloody Hand............................. 14
A Summary History of Lord Clive 18
The Battle of the Nile 21
Beautiful Aberfoyle................................... 23
The Convict's Return 27
The Battle of Alexandria, or the Reconquest of Egypt 28
Saved by Music 31
Beautiful Newport on the Braes o' the Silvery Tay.......... 34
The Battle of Corunna................................ 35
A Tale of Christmas Eve 37
The Battle of Gujrat.................................. 39
Bill Bowls the Sailor.................................. 42
The Battle of the Alma, fought in 1854.................... 44
Beautiful Rothesay.................................... 47
The Battle of Inkermann............................... 48
Little Pierre's Song 51
The Capture of Lucknow 52
The Burns Statue..................................... 58
The Hero of Kalapore: an Incident of the Indian Mutiny 59
Jack Honest, or the Widow and her Son.................... 62
The Downfall of Delhi................................. 66
The River of Leith.................................... 69
The Ashantee War: the Fall of Coomassie 71
The Beautiful City of Perth............................ 74
General Roberts in Afghanistan 76
Requistion to the Queen 79

FAREWELL ADDRESS AT THE ARGYLE HALL, TUESDAY, JUNE 22, 1880

Fellow Citizens of Dundee.
I now must bid farewell to ye.
For I am going to London far away.
But when I will return again I cannot say.

Farewell! Farewell! to the bonnie banks o' the Silvery Tay.
Also the beautiful Hill o' Balgay.
And the ill fated Bridge o' the Silvery Tay.
Which I will remember when I am far away.

Farewell! to my friends and patrons all.
That rallied around me in the Music Hall.
And those that has rallied around me to night,
I shall not forget when out of sight.

And if I ever return to Dundee again,
I hope it will be with the laurels of fame.
Plac'd on my brow by dame fortune that fickle Jade.
And to Court her favour I am not afraid.

Farewell! to every one in the Argyle Hall.
That has Come to hear McGonagall.
Recite, and sing, his Songs to night.
Which I hope will long be remember'd when I'm out of
    sight.

Adieu to all my enemies that want to mock me when
    passing by.
But I excuse them for their ignorance and leave them to
    the most high.
And, once again, my friends, and enemies. I bid ye all
    good bye.
And when I am gone ye will for me heave a sigh: —

7

I return my thanks to my Chairman and my Committee,
For the Kindness they have always shown to me.
I hope the Lord! will protect them when I am far away.
And prosper them in all their undertakings by night and
　by day.

THE LAST BERKSHIRE ELEVEN:
THE HEROES OF MAIWAND

'Twas at the disastrous battle of Maiwand, in Afghanistan,
Where the Berkshires were massacred to the last man;
On the morning of July the 27th, in the year eighteen
　eighty,
Which I'm sorry to relate was a pitiful sight to see.

Ayoub Khan's army amounted to twelve thousand in all,
And honestly speaking it wasn't very small,
And by such a great force the Berkshires were killed to the
　last man,
By a murderous rebel horde under the command of Ayoub
　Khan.

The British force amounted to about 2000 strong in all,
But although their numbers were but few it didn't them
　appal;
They were commanded by General Burrows, a man of
　courage bold,
But, alas! the British army was defeated be it told.

The 66th Berkshire Regiment stood as firm as a wall,
Determined to conquer or die whatever would befall,
But in the face of overwhelming odds, and covered to the
    last,
The broken and disordered Sepoys were flying fast

Before the victorious Afghan soldiers, whose cheers on the
    air arose,
But the gallant band poured in deadly volleys on their foes;
And, outnumbered and surrounded, they fell in sections like
    ripe grain;
Still the heroes held their ground, charging with might and
    main.

The British force, alas! were shut up like sheep in a pen,
Owing to the bad position General Burrows had chosen for
    his men;
But Colonel Galbraith with the Berkshires held the enemy
    at bay,
And had the Sepoys been rallied the Afghans would not
    have won the day.

But on the Berkshires fell the brunt of the battle,
For by the Afghan artillery they fell like slaughtered
    cattle;
Yet the wild horsemen were met with ringing volleys of
    musketry,
Which emptied many a saddle; still the Afghans fought
    right manfully.

And on came the white cloud like a whirlwind;
But the gallant Berkshires, alas! no help could find,
While their blood flowed like water on every side around,
And they fell in scores, but the men rallied and held their
    ground.

The brave Berkshires under Colonel Galbraith stood firm in
  the centre there,
Whilst the shouts of the wild Ghazis rent the air;
But still the Berkshires held them at bay,
At the charge of the bayonet, without dismay.

Then the Ghazis, with increased numbers, made another
  desperate charge
On that red line of British bayonets, which wasn't very
  large;
And the wild horsemen were met again with ringing volleys
  of musketry,
Which was most inspiring and frightful to see.

Then Ayoub concentrated his whole attack on the Berkshire
  Regiment,
Which made them no doubt feel rather discontent,
And Jacob's Rifles and the Grenadiers were a confused and
  struggling mass,
Oh heaven! such a confused scene, nothing could it surpass.

But the Berkshires stood firm, replying to the fire of the
  musketry,
While they were surrounded on all sides by masses of
  cavalry;
Still that gallant band resolved to fight for their Queen and
  country,
Their motto being death before dishonour, rather than flee.

At last the gallant British soldiers made a grand stand,
While most of the officers were killed fighting hand to hand,
And at length the Sepoys fled from the enclosure, panic-stricken
  and irate,
Alas! leaving behind their European comrades to their fate.

The Berkshires were now reduced to little more than one
hundred men,
Who were huddled together like sheep in a pen;
But they broke loose from the enclosure, and back to back,
Poured volley after volley in the midst of the enemy, who
wern't slack.

And one by one they fell, still the men fought without
dismay,
And the regimental pet dog stuck to the heroes throughtout
the day;
And their cartridge pouches were empty, and of shot they
were bereft,
And eleven men, most of them wounded, were all that were
left.

Oh, heaven! it was a fearful scene the horrors of that
day,
When I think of so many innocent lives that were taken
away;
Alas! the British force were massacred in cold blood,
And their blood ran like a little rivulet in full flood.

And the Ghazis were afraid to encounter that gallant little
band
At the charge of the bayonet: Oh! the scene was most
grand;
And the noble and heroic eleven fought on without dismay,
Until the last man in the arms of death stiff and stark lay.

THE DEMON DRINK

Oh, thou demon Drink, thou fell destroyer;
Thou curse of society, and its greatest annoyer.
What hast thou done to society, let me think?
I answer thou hast caused the most of ills, thou demon
   Drink.

Thou causeth the mother to neglect her child,
Also the father to act as he were wild,
So that he neglects his loving wife and family dear,
By spending his earnings foolishly on whisky, rum, and beer.

And after spending his earnings foolishly he beats his wife—
The man that promised to protect her during life—
And so the man would if there was no drink in society,
For seldom a man beats his wife in a state of sobriety.

And if he does, perhaps he finds his wife fou,'
Then that causes, no doubt, a great hullaballoo;
When he finds his wife drunk he begins to frown,
And in a fury of passion he knocks her down.

And in the knock down she fractures her head,
And perhaps the poor wife is killed dead,
Whereas, if there was no strong drink to be got,
To be killed wouldn't have been the poor wife's lot.

Then the unfortunate husband is arrested and cast into jail,
And sadly his fate he does bewail;
And he curses the hour that ever he was born,
And paces his cell up and down very forlorn.

And when the day of his trial draws near,
No doubt for the murdering of his wife he drops a tear,
And he exclaims, "Oh, thou demon Drink, through thee I
    must die,"
And on the scaffold he warns the people from drink to fly,

Because whenever a father or a mother takes to drink,
Step by step on in crime they do sink,
Until their children loses all affection for them,
And in justice we cannot their children condemn.

The man that gets drunk is little else than a fool,
And is in the habit, no doubt, of advocating for Home Rule;
But the best Home Rule for him, as far as I can understand,
Is the abolition of strong drink from the land.

And the men that get drunk in general wants Home Rule;
But such men, I rather think should keep their heads cool,
And try and learn more sense, I most earnestly do pray,
And help to get strong drink abolished without delay.

If drink was abolished how many peaceful homes would
    there be,
Just, for instance, in the beautiful town of Dundee;
Then this world would be a heaven, whereas it's a hell,
And the people would have more peace in it to dwell.

Alas! strong drink makes men and women fanatics,
And helps to fill our prisons and lunatics;
And if there was no strong drink such cases wouldn't be,
Which would be a very glad sight for all Christians to see.

I admit, a man may be a very good man,
But in my opinion he cannot be a true Christian
As long as he partakes of strong drink,
The more that he may differently think.

But, no matter what he thinks, I say nay,
For by taking it he helps to lead his brother astray,
Whereas, if he didn't drink, he would help to reform society,
And we would soon do away with all inebriety.

Then, for the sake of society and the Church of God,
Let each one try to abolish it at home and abroad;
Then poverty and crime would decrease and be at a stand,
And Christ's Kingdom would soon be established throughout
    the land.

Therefore, brothers and sisters, pause and think,
And try to abolish the foul fiend, Drink.
Let such doctrine be taught in church and school,
That the abolition of strong drink is the only Home Rule.

GRIF, OF THE BLOODY HAND

In an immense wood in the south of Kent,
There lived a band of robbers which caused the people
    discontent;
And the place they infested was called the Weald,
Where they robbed wayside travellers and left them dead on
    the field.

Their leader was called Grif, of the Bloody Hand,
And so well skilled in sword practice there's few could him
    withstand;
And sometimes they robbed villages when nothing else
    could be gained,
In the year of 1336, when King Edward the III. reigned.

The dress the robbers wore was deep coloured black,
And in courage and evil deeds they didn't lack;
And Grif, of the Bloody Hand, called them his devils,
Because they were ever ready to perform all kinds of ills.

"Twas towards the close of a very stormy day,
A stranger walked through the wood in search of Grif,
    without dismay;
And as the daylight faded he quickened his pace and ran,
Never suspecting that in his rear he was followed by a man.

And as the man to the stranger drew near,
He demanded in a gruff voice, what seek you here;
And when the stranger saw him he trembled with fear,
Because upon his head he wore a steel helmet, and in his
    hand he bore a spear.

What seek you here repeated the dark habited man,
Come, sir, speak out, and answer me if you can;
Are you then one of the devils demanded the stranger
    faintly,
That I am said the man, now what matters that to thee.

Then repeated the stranger, sir, you have put me to a stand,
But if I guess aright, you are Grif, of the Bloody Hand;
That I am replied Grif, and to confess it I'm not afraid,
Oh! well then I require your service and you'll be well paid.

15

But first I must know thy name, I, that's the point,
Then you shall have the help of my band conjoint;
Before any of my men on your mission goes,
Well then replied the stranger call me Martin Dubois.

Well sir, come tell me what you want as quick as you can,
Well then replied Dubois do you know one Halbert Evesham
That dwells in the little village of Brenchley,
Who has a foster child called Violet Evesham of rare beauty.

And you seek my aid to carry her off,
Ha! ha! a love affair, nay do not think I scoff;
For you shall enjoy her sir before this time to morrow,
If that will satisfy you, or help to drown your sorrow.

And now sir what is your terms with me,
Before I carry off Violet Evesham from the village of
    Brenchley;
Well Grif, one thousand marks shall be the pay,
'Tis agreed then cried Grif, and you shall enjoy her without
    delay.

Then the bargains struck, uttered Grif, how many men will
    you require,
Come sir, speak, you can have all my band if you desire;
Oh, thanks sir, replied Dubois, I consider four men will do,
That's to say sir if the four men's courage be true.

And to-morrow sir send the men to Brenchley without delay,
And remember one thousand merks will be the pay;
And the plan I propose is to carry her to the wood,
And I will be there to receive her, the plan is good.

And on the next morning Grif, of the Bloody Hand,
Told off four of his best men and gave them strict command;
To carry off Violet Evesham from the village of Brenchley,
And to go about it fearlessly and make no delay.

And when ye have captured her carry her to the wood,
Now remember men I wish my injunctions to be understood;
All right, captain, we'll do as we've be told,
And carry her off all right for the sake of the gold.

So on the next morning before the villagers were out of bed,
The four robbers marched into the village of Brenchley
    without any dread;
And boldly entered Violet Evesham's house and carried her,
    away,
While loudly the beautiful girl shrieked in dismay.

But when her old father missed her through the village he
    ran,
And roused the villagers to a man;
And a great number of them gathered, and Wat Tyler at
    their head,
And all armed to the teeth, and towards the wood they
    quickly sped.

And once within the wood Wat Tyler cried, where is Violet
    Evesham,
Then Grif, of the Bloody Hand cried, what ails the man;
My dear sir I assure you that Violet Evesham is not here.
Therefore good people I advise ye to retire from here.

No! I'll not back cried Wat Tyler, until I rescue Violet
    Evesham,
Therefore liar, and devil, defend thyself if you can;
Ay replied Grif, that I will thou braggart loon,
And with my sword you silly boy prepare for thy doom.

Then they rained their blows on each other as thick as hail,
Until at last Grif's strength began to fail;
Then Wat leaped upon him and threw him to the ground,
Then his men fled into the wood that were standing around.

Then the villagers shouted hurrah for Wat Tyler and
    victory,
And to search for Violet Evesham they willingly did agree;
And they searched the wood and found her at the foot of a
    tree,
And when she was taken home the villagers danced with
    glee.

And 'tis said Wat Tyler married Violet Evesham,
And there was great rejoicing among the villagers at the
    marriage so grand;
And Wat Tyler captured Dubois, and bound him to a tree,
And left him there struggling hard to gain his liberty.

A SUMMARY HISTORY OF LORD CLIVE

About a hundred and fifty years ago,
History relates it happened so,
A big ship sailed from the shores of Britain
Bound for India across the raging main.

And many of the passengers did cry and moan
As they took the last look of their old home,
Which they were fast leaving far behind,
And which some of them would long bear in mind.

Among the passengers was a youth about seventeen years
 old,
Who had been a wild boy at home and very bold,
And by his conduct had filled his parents' hearts with woe,
Because to school he often refused to go.

And now that he was going so far away from home,
The thought thereof made him sigh and groan,
For he felt very sad and dejected were his looks,
And he often wished he had spent more time at his books.

And when he arrived in India he searched for work there,
And got to be clerk in a merchant's office, but for it he didn't
 care;
The only pleasure he found was in reading books,
And while doing so, sad and forlorn were his looks.

One day while feeling unhappy he fired a pistol at his own
 head,
Expecting that he would kill himself dead;
But the pistol wouldn't go off although he tried every plan,
And he felt sorry, and resolved to become a better man.

So Clive left his desk and became a soldier brave,
And soon rose to be a captain and manfully did behave;
For he beat the French in every battle,
After all their foolish talk and prattle.

Then he thought he would take a voyage home to his friends,
And for his bad behaviour towards them he would make
   some amends;
For he hadn't seen them for many years,
And when he thought of them he shed briny tears.

And when he arrived in London
The people after him in crowds did run;
And they flocked to see him every minute,
Because they thought him the most famous man in it.

And all the greatest people in the land
Were proud to shake him by the hand;
And they gave him a beautiful sword because he had fought
   so well
And of his bravery the people to each other did tell.

And when his own friends saw him they to him ran,
And they hardly knew him, he looked so noble a man;
And his parents felt o'erjoyed when they saw him home
   again,
And when he left his parents again for India it caused them
   great pain.

But it was a good thing Clive returned to India again,
Because a wicked prince in his territory wouldn't allow the
   British to remain,
And he resolved to drive them off his land,
And marched upon them boldly with thousands of his band

But the bad prince trembled when he heard that Clive had
    come,
Because the British at the charge of the bayonet made his
    army run;
And the bad prince was killed by one of his own band,
And the British fortunately got all his land.

And nearly all India now belongs to this country,
Which has been captured by land and by sea,
By some of the greatest men that ever did live,
But the greatest of them all was Robert Clive.

THE BATTLE OF THE NILE

'Twas on the 18th of August in the year of 1798,
That Nelson saw with inexpressible delight
The City of Alexandria crowded with the ships of France,
So he ordered all sail to be set, and immediately advance.

And upon the deck, in deep anxiety he stood,
And from anxiety of mind he took but little food;
But now he ordered dinner to be prepared without delay,
Saying, I shall gain a peerage to-morrow, or Westminster
    Abbey.

The French had found it impossible to enter the port of
    Alexandria,
Therefore they were compelled to withdraw;
Yet their hearts were burning with anxiety the war to begin,
But they couldn't find a pilot who would convey them
    safely in.

Therefore Admiral Brueys was forced to anchor in Aboukir
    Bay,
And in a compact line of battle, the leading vessel lay
Close to a shoal, along a line of very deep water,
There they lay, all eager to begin the murderous slaughter.

The French force consisted of thirteen ships of the line,
As fine as ever sailed on the salt sea brine;
Besides four Frigates carrying 1,196 guns in all,
Also 11,230 men as good as ever fired a cannon ball.

The number of the English ships were thirteen in all,
And carrying 1012 guns, including great and small;
And the number of the men were 8,068,
All jolly British tars and eager for to fight.

As soon as Nelson perceived the position of the enemy,
His active mind soon formed a plan immediately;
As the plan he thought best, as far as he could see,
Was to anchor his ships on the quarter of each of the enemy.

And when he had explained his mode of attack to his officers
    and men,
He said, form as convenient, and anchor at the stern;
Then first gain the victory, and make the best use of it you
    can,
Therefore I hope every one here to-day, will do their duty to
    a man.

When Captain Berry perceived the boldness of the plan,
He said, my Lord, I'm sure the men will do their duty to a
    man;
And, my Lord, what will the world say, if we gain the
    victory?
Then Nelson replied, there's no if in the case, and that you'll
    see.

Then the British tars went to work without delay,
All hurrying to and fro, making ready for the fray;
And there wasn't a man among them, but was confident
  that day,
That they would make the French to fly from Aboukir Bay.

Nelson's Fleet did not enter Aboukir Bay at once,
And by adopting that plan, that was his only chance;
But one after another, they bore down on the enemy;
Then Nelson cried, now open fire my heroes, immediately!

Then the shores of Egypt trembled with the din of the war,
While sheets of flame rent the thick clouds afar;
And the contending fleets hung incumbent o'er the bay,
Whilst our British tars stuck to their guns without the least
  dismay.

And loudly roared the earthly thunder along the river Nile,
And the British ship Orion went into action in splendid
    style;
Also Nelson's Ship Vanguard bore down on the foe,
With six flags flying from her rigging high and low.

Then she opened a tremendous fire on the Spartiate,
And Nelson cried, fear not my lads we'll soon make them
  retreat!
But so terrific was the fire of the enemy on them,
That six of the Vanguards guns were cleared of men.

Yet there stood Nelson, the noble Hero of the Nile,
In the midst of death and destruction on deck all the while;
And around him on every side, the cannon balls did rattle,
But right well the noble hero knew the issue of the battle.

But suddenly he received a wound on the head,
And fell into the arms of Captain Berry, but fortunately not
    dead;
And the flow of blood from his head was very great,
But still the hero of the Nile was resigned to his fate.

Then to the Cockpit the great Admiral was carried down,
And in the midst of the dying, he never once did frown;
Nor he did'nt shake with fear, nor yet did he mourne,
But patiently sat down to wait his own turn.

And when the Surgeon saw him, he instantly ran,
But Nelson said, Surgeon, attend to that man;
Attend to the sailor you were at, for he requires your aid,
Then I will take my turn, don't be the least afraid.

And when his turn came, it was found that his wound was
    but slight,
And when known, it filled the sailors hearts with delight;
And they all hoped he would soon be able to command in the
    fight,
When suddenly a cry arose of fire! which startled Nelson
    with affright.

And unassisted he rushed upon the deck, and to his amaze,
He discovered that the Orient was all in a blaze;
Then he ordered the men to lower the boats, and relieve the
    enemy,
Saying, now men, see and obey my orders immediately.

Then the noble tars manned their boats, and steered to the
    Orient,
While the poor creatures thanked God for the succour He
    had sent;
And the burning fragments fell around them like rain,
Still our British tars rescued about seventy of them from the
    burning flame,

And of the thirteen sail of the French the British captured
    nine,
Besides four of their ships were burnt, which made the scene
    sublime,
Which made the hero of the Nile cry out thank God we've
    won the day,
And defeated the French most manfully in Aboukir Bay.

Then the victory was complete and the French fleet
    annihilated,
And when the news arrived in England the peoples' hearts
    felt elated,
Then Nelson sent orders immediately through the fleet,
That thanksgiving should be returned to God for the victory
    complete.

BEAUTIFUL ABERFOYLE

The mountains and glens of Aberfoyle are beautiful to sight,
Likewise the rivers and lakes are sparkling and bright;
And its woods were frequented by the Lady of the Lake,
And on its Lakes many a sail in her boat she did take.

The scenery there will fill the tourist with joy,
Because 'tis there once lived the bold Rob Roy,
Who spent many happy days with his Helen there,
By chasing the deer in the woods so fair.

The little vale of Aberfoyle and its beautiful river
Is a sight, once seen, forget it you'll never;
And romantic ranges of rock on either side
Form a magnificent background far and wide.

And the numerous lochs there abound with trout
Which can be had for the taking out,
Especially from the Lochs Chon and Ard,
There the angler can make a catch which will his toil reward.

And between the two lochs the Glasgow Water Works are
    near,
Which convey water of Loch Katrine in copious streams
    clear
To the inhabitants of the Great Metropolis of the West,
And for such pure water they should think themselves blest.

The oak and birch woods there are beautiful to view,
Also the Ochil hills which are blue in hue,
Likewise the Lake of Menteith can be seen far eastward,
Also Stirling Castle, which long ago the English besieged
    very hard.

Then away to Aberfoyle, Rob Roy's country,
And gaze on the magnificent scenery.
A region of rivers and mountains towering majestically
Which is lovely and fascinating to see.

But no words can describe the beautiful scenery.
Aberfoyle must be visited in order to see,
So that the mind may apprehend its beauties around,
Which will charm the hearts of the visitors I'll be bound.

As for the clachan of Aberfoyle, little remains but a hotel,
Which for accommodation will suit the traveller very well.
And the bedding there is clean and good,
And good cooks there to cook the food.

Then away to the mountains and lakes of bonnie Aberfoyle,
Ye hard-working sons and daughters of daily toil;
And traverse its heathery mountains and view its lakes so
    clear,
When the face of Nature's green in the spring of the year.

THE CONVICT'S RETURN

Ye mountains and glens of fair Scotland I'm with ye once
    again,
During my absence from ye my heart was like to break in
    twain;
Oh! how I longed to see you and the old folks at home,
And with my lovely Jeannie once more in the green woods
    to roam.

Now since I've returned safe home again
I will try and be content
With my lovely Jeannie at home,
And forget my banishment.

27

My Jeannie and me will get married,
And I will be to her a good man,
And we'll live happy together,
And do the best we can.

I hope my Jeannie and me
Will always happy be,
And never feel discontent;
And at night at the fireside
I'll relate to her the trials of my banishment.

But now I will never leave my Jeannie again
Until the day I die;
And before the vital spark has fled
I will bid ye all good-bye.

THE BATTLE OF ALEXANDRIA, OR THE RECONQUEST OF EGYPT

It was on the 21st of March in the year of 1801,
The British were at their posts every man;
And their position was naturally very strong,
And the whole line from sea to lake was about a mile long.

And on the ruins of a Roman Palace, rested the right,
And every man amongst them was eager for the fight,
And the reserve was under the command of Major General
    Moore,
A hero brave, whose courage was both firm and sure.

And in the valley between the right were the cavalry,
Which was really a most beautiful sight to see;
And the 28th were posted in a redoubt open in the rear,
Determined to hold it to the last without the least fear.

And the Guards and the Inniskillings were eager for the fray,
Also the Gordon Highlanders and Cameron Highlanders in
    grand array;
Likewise the dismounted Cavalry and the noble dragoons,
Who never fear'd the cannons shot when it loudly booms.

And between the two armies stretched a sandy plain,
Which the French tried to chase the British off, but it was
    all in vain,
And a more imposing battle-field seldom has been chosen,
But alack the valour of the French soon got frozen.

Major General Moore was the general officer of the night,
And had galloped off to the left and to the right,
The instant he heard the enemy briskly firing;
He guessed by their firing they had no thought of retiring.

Then a wild broken huzza was heard from the plain below,
And followed by a rattle of musketry from the foe;
Then the French advanced in column with their drums
    loudly beating,
While their officers cried forward men and no retreating.

Then the colonel of the 58th reserved his fire,
Until the enemy drew near, which was his desire;
Then he ordered his men to attack them from behind the
    palace wall,
Then he opened fire at thirty yards, which did the enemy
    appal.

And thus assailed in front, flank, and rear,
The French soon began to shake with fear;
Then the 58th charged them with the bayonet, with courage
  unshaken,
And all the enemy that entered the palace ruins were killed
  or taken.

Then the French Invincibles, stimulated by liquor and the
  promise of gold,
Stole silently along the valley with tact and courage bold,
Proceeded by a 6 pounder gun, between the right of the
  guards,
But brave Lieutenant-Colonel Stewart quickly their
  progress retards.

Then Colonel Stewart cried to the right wing,
Forward! my lads, and make the valley ring,
And charge them with your bayonets and capture their gun,
And before very long they will be glad to run.

Then loudly grew the din of battle, like to rend the skies,
As major Stirling's left wing faced, and charged them
  likewise;
Then the Invincibles maddened by this double attack,
Dashed forward on the palace ruins, but they soon were
  driven back.

And by the 58th, and Black Watch they were brought to
  bay, here,
But still they were resolved to sell their lives most dear,
And it was only after 650 of them had fallen in the fray,
That the rest threw down their arms and quickly ran away.

Then unexpected, another great body of the enemy was seen,
With their banners waving in the breeze, most beautiful and
   green;
And advancing on the left of the redoubt,
But General Moore instantly ordered the Black Watch out.

And he cried, brave Highlanders you are always in the
   hottest of the fight,
Now make ready for the bayonet charge with all your might;
And remember our country and your forefathers
As soon as the enemy and ye foregathers.

Then the Black Watch responded with a loud shout,
And charged them with their bayonots without fear or
   doubt;
And the French tried hard to stand the charge, but it was all
   in vain,
And in confussion they all fled across the sandy plain.

Oh! it was a glorious victory, the British gained that day,
But the joy of it, alas! was unfortunately taken away,
Because Sir Ralph Abercrombie, in the hottest of the fight,
   was shot,
And for his undaunted bravery, his name will never be
   forgot.

SAVED BY MUSIC

At one time, in America, many years ago,
Large gray wolves wont to wander to and fro;
And from the farm yards they carried pigs and calves away,
Which they devoured ravenously, without dismay.

31

But, as the story goes, there was a negro fiddler called old
   Dick,
Who was invited by a wedding party to give them music,
In the winter time, when the snow lay thick upon the ground
And the rivers far and near were frozen all around.

So away went Dick to the wedding as fast as he could go,
Walking cautiously along o'er the crisp and crackling snowm,
And the path was a narrow one, the greater part of the way
Through a dark forest, which filled his heart with dismay.

And when hurrying onward, not to be late at the festival,
He heard the howl of a wolf, which did his heart appal,
And the howl was answered, and as the howl came near
Poor Old Dick, fiddle in hand, began to shake with fear.

And as the wolves gathered in packs from far and near,
Old Dick in the crackling bushes did them hear,
And they ran along to keep pace with him,
Then poor Dick began to see the danger he was in.

And every few minutes a wolf would rush past him with a
   snap,
With a snapping sound like the ring of a steel trap,
And the pack of wolves gathered with terrible rapidity,
So that Dick didn't know whether to stand or flee.

And his only chance, he thought, was to keep them at bay
By preserving the greatest steadiness without dismay,
Until he was out of the forest and on open ground,
Where he thought a place of safety might be found.

He remembered an old hut stood in the clearing,
And towards it he was slowly nearing,
And the hope of reaching it urged him on,
But he felt a trifle dispirited and woe-begone.

And the poor fellow's heart with fear gave a bound,
When he saw the wolves' green eyes glaring all around,
And they rushed at him boldly, one after another,
Snapping as they passed, which to him was great bother.

And Dick sounded his fiddle and tried to turn them back,
And the sound caused the wolves to leap back in a crack,
When Dick took to his heels at full run,
But now poor Dick's danger was only begun:

For the wolves pursued him without delay,
But Dick arrived at the hut in great dismay,
And had just time to get on the roof and play,
And at the strains of the music the wolves felt gay.

And for several hours he sat there in pain,
Knowing if he stopped playing the wolves would be at him
    again,
But the rage of the wolves abated to the subduing strains,
And at last he was rewarded for all his pains:

For the wedding-party began to weary for some music,
And they all came out to look for Old Dick,
And on the top of the hut they found him fiddling away,
And they released him from his dangerous position without
    delay.

BEAUTIFUL NEWPORT ON THE BRAES
O' THE SILVERY TAY

Bonnie Mary, the Maid o' the Tay,
Come! let's go, and have a holiday
In Newport, on the braes o' the silvery Tay,
'Twill help to drive dull care away.

The scenery there is most enchanting to be seen,
Especially the fine mansions with their shrubbery green;
And the trees and ivy are beautiful to view
Growing in front of each stately home in the avenue.

There the little birds and beautiful butterflies
Are soaring heavenwards almost to the skies,
And the busy bees are to be seen on the wing,
As from flower to flower they hummingly sing,

As they gather honey all the day,
From the flowery gardens of Newport on the braes o' the
    Tay.
And as we view the gardens our hearts will feel gay
After being pent up in the workshop all the day.

Then there's a beautiful spot near an old mill,
Suitable for an artist to paint of great skill,
And the trees are arched o'erhead, lovely to be seen,
Which screens ye from the sunshine's glittering sheen.

Therefore, holiday makers, I'd have ye resort
To Newport on the braes o' the Tay for sport,
And inhale the pure air with its sweet perfume,
Emanating from the flowery gardens of Newport and the
    yellow broom.

And when bright Sol sinks in the West
You'll return home at night quite refreshed,
And dream in your beds of your rambles during the day
Along the bonnie braes o' the silvery Tay.

THE BATTLE OF CORUNNA

'Twas in the year of 1808, and in the autumn of the year,
Napoleon resolved to crush Spain and Portugal without fear;
So with a mighty army three hundred thousand strong
Through the passes of the Pyrenees into Spain he passed
  along.

But Sir John Moore concentrated his troops in the north,
And into the west corner of Spain he boldly marched forth;
To cut off Napoleon's communications with France
He considered it to be advisable and his only chance.

And when Napoleon heard of Moore's coming, his march he
  did begin,
Declaring that he was the only General that could oppose
  him;
And in the month of December, when the hills were clad
  with snow,
Napoleon's army marched over the Guadiana Hills with
  their hearts full of woe.

And with fifty thousand cavalry, infantry, and artillery,
Napoleon marched on, facing obstacles most dismal to see;
And performed one of the most rapid marches recorded in
  history,
Leaving the command of his army to Generals Soult and
  Ney.

And on the 5th of January Soult made his attack
But in a very short time the French were driven back;
With the Guards and the 50th Regiment and the 42d
    conjoint,
They were driven from the village of Elnina at the bayonet's
    point.

Oh! it was a most gorgeous and inspiring sight
To see Sir John Moore in the thickest of the fight,
And crying aloud to the 42d with all his might;
"Forward, my lads, and charge them with your bayonets
    left and right."

Then the 42d charged them with might and main,
And the French were repulsed again and again;
And although they poured into the British ranks a withering
    fire,
The British at the charge of the bayonet soon made them
    retire.

Oh! that battlefield was a fearful sight to behold,
'Twas enough to make one's blood run cold
To hear the crack, crack of the musketry and the cannon's
    roar,
Whilst the dead and the dying lay weltering in their gore.

But O Heaven! it was a heartrending sight,
When Sir John Moore was shot dead in the thickest of the
    fight;
And as the soldiers bore him from the field they looked
    woebegone,
And the hero's last words were "Let me see how the battle
    goes on."

Then he breathed his last with a gurgling sound,
And for the loss of the great hero the soldiers' sorrow was
    profound,
Because he was always kind and served them well,
And as they thought of him tears down their cheeks trickling
    fell.

Oh! it was a weird and pathetic sight
As they buried him in the Citadel of Corunna at the dead of
    night,
While his staff and the men shed many tears
For the noble hero who had commanded them for many
    years.

Success to the British Army wherever they go,
For seldom they have failed to conquer the foe;
Long may the Highlanders be able to make the foe reel,
By giving them an inch or two of cold steel.

A TALE OF CHRISTMAS EVE

'Twas Christmastide in Germany,
And in the year of 1850,
And in the city of Berlin, which is most beautiful to the eye;
A poor boy was heard calling out to the passers-by.

"Who'll buy my pretty figures," loudly he did cry,
Plaster of Paris figures, but no one inclined to buy;
His clothes were thin and he was nearly frozen with cold,
And wholly starving with hunger, a pitiful sight to behold.

And the twilight was giving place to the shadows of
    approaching night,
And those who possessed a home were seeking its warmth
    and light;
And the market square was dark and he began to moan,
When he thought of his hungry brother and sisters at home.

Alas! the poor boy was afraid to go home,
Oh, Heaven! hard was his lot, for money he'd none;
And the tears coursed down his cheeks while loudly he did
    cry,
"Buy my plaster of Paris figures, oh! please come buy."

It was now quite dark while he stood there,
And the passers-by did at the poor boy stare,
As he stood shivering with cold in the market square;
And with the falling snow he was almost frozen to the bone.
And what would it avail him standing there alone,
Therefore he must make up his mind to return home.

Then he tried to hoist the board and figures on to his head,
And for fear of letting the board fall he was in great dread;
Then he struggled manfully forward without delay,
But alas! he fell on the pavement, oh! horror and dismay.

And his beautiful figures were broken and scattered around
    him,
And at the sight thereof his eyes grew dim;
And when he regained his feet he stood speechless like one
    bowed down,
Then the poor boy did fret and frown.

Then the almost despairing boy cried aloud,
And related his distress to the increasing crowd;
Oh! What a pitiful sight on a Christmas eve,
But the dense crowd didn't the poor boy relieve,

Until a poor wood-cutter chanced to come along,
And he asked of the crowd what was wrong;
And twenty ready tongues tells him the sad tale,
And when he heard it the poor boy's fate he did bewail.

And he cried, "Here! Something must be done and quickly
    too,
Do you hear! Every blessed soul of you;
Come, each one give a few pence to the poor boy,
And it will help to fill his heart with joy."

Then the wood-cutter gave a golden coin away,
So the crowd subscribed largely without delay;
Which made the poor boy's heart feel gay,
Then the wood-cutter thanked the crowd and went away.

So the poor boy did a large subscription receive,
And his brother, mother, and sisters had a happy Christmas
    eve;
And he thanked the crowd and God that to him the money
    sent.
And bade the crowd good-night, then went home content.

THE BATTLE OF GUJRAT

'Twas in the year of 1849, and on the 20th of February,
Lord Gough met and attacked Shere Sing right manfully.
The Sikh Army numbered 40,000 in strength,
And showing a front about two miles length.

It was a glorious morning, the sun was shining in a cloudless
   sky;
And the larks were singing merrily in the heavens high;
And 'twas about nine o'clock in the morning the battle was
   begun,
But at the end of three hours the Sikhs were forced to run.

Lord Gough's force was a mixture of European and native
   infantry,
And well supported with artillery and cavalry;
But the British Army in numbers weren't so strong,
Yet, fearlessly and steadily, they marched along.

Shere Sing, the King, had taken up a position near the town,
And as he gazed upon the British Army he did frown;
But Lord Gough ordered the troops to commence the battle,
With sixty big guns that loudly did rattle.

The Sikhs were posted on courses of deep water,
But the British in a short time soon did them scatter.
Whilst the British cannonading loudly bums,
And in the distance were heard the enemy's drums.

Then the Sikhs began to fight with their artillery,
But their firing didn't work very effectively;
Then the British lines advanced on them right steadily,
Which was a most inspiring sight to see.

Then the order was given to move forward to attack,
And again — and again — through fear the enemy drew back.
Then Penny's brigade, with a ringing cheer, advanced
   briskly,
And charged with their bayonets very heroically.

Then the Sikhs caught the bayonets with their left hand,
And rushed in with their swords, the scene was heroic and
  grand.
Whilst they slashed and cut with great dexterity,
But the British charge was irresistible, they had to flee.

And with 150 men they cleared the village of every living
  thing,
And with British cheers the village did ring;
And the villagers in amazement and terror fled,
Because the streets and their houses were strewn with their
  dead.

The chief attack was made on the enemy's right
By Colin Campbell's brigade – a most magnificent sight.
Though they were exposed to a very galling fire,
But at last the Sikhs were forced to retire.

And in their flight everthing was left behind,
And the poor Sikhs were of all comfort bereft,
Because their swords, cannon, drums, and waggons were left
  behind,
Therefore little pleasure could they find.

Then Shere Sing fled in great dismay,
But Lord Gough pursued him without delay,
And captured him a few miles away;
And now the Sikhs are our best soldiers of the present day,
Because India is annexed to the British Dominions, and they
  must obey.

BILL BOWLS THE SAILOR

Bill Bowels was an amiable gentle youth,
And concerning him I'll relate the truth;
His Mother wanted to make him a Tailor,
But Bill's Father said he was cut out for a Sailor.

Dancing bareheaded under heavy rain was his delight,
And wading in ponds and rivers by day and night;
And he was as full of mischief as an Egg is full of meat,
And tumbling and swimming in deep pools to him was a
    treat.

His Father was a Mill Wright, and lived near a small lake,
And many a swim in that lake, Bill used to take;
And many a good lesson his good dad gave to him,
To keep always in shoal water till he could swim.

One day he got hold of a very big plank,
And with it he resolved to play some funny prank,
So he launched the plank into the lake,
Crying now I'll have some rare fun and no mistake.

And on the plank he went with a piece broken paling for an
    oar,
But suddenly a squall came down on the lake which made
    him roar,
And threw him on his beam ends into the water,
And the clothes he had on him were drenched every tatter.

'Twas lucky for Bill his Father heard his cries,
And to save poor Bill he instantly flies,
And he leaped into the lake and dragged Bill ashore,
While Bill for help did lustily roar.

Then after that he joined a ship bound for China,
With a pair of light breeches and his heart full of glee,
But his heart soon became less buoyant
When he discovered his Captain was a great tyrant.

One evening as Bill stood talking to the steersman,
And the weather at the time was very calm;
Tom Riggles said, Bill we're going to have dirty weather,
But with the help of God, we'll weather it together.

That night the Captain stood holding to on the shrouds,
While scudding across the sky were thick angry clouds
And the ship was running unsteady before the wind,
And the Captain was drunk must be borne in mind.

Then a cry is heard which might have chilled the stoutest
    heart,
Which caused every man on board with fear to start;
Oh! heavens, rocks ahead, shouted the mate, above the gale,
While every face on board turned ghastly pale.

Then, port! port! hard-a-port! shouted the men
All over the ship, from bow to stern,
And the order was repeated by the mate
Who sprang to the wheel, fearlessly resigned to his fate.

At last a heavy wave struck the ship with a terrible dash,
Which made every plank quiver and give way with a crash,
While wave on the back of wave struck her with fearful
    shocks,
Until at last she was lifted up and cast on the rugged rocks.

Oh! heaven, it must have been an awful sight,
To witness in the dusky moon-light;
Men clinging to the rigging with all their might,
And others trying to put the ship all right.

Then the wind it blew a terrific blast,
Which tore the rigging away and the missen-mast;
And the big waves lashed her furiously,
And the Captain was swept with the wreck into the sea.

Then every man struggled manfully to gain the shore,
While the storm fiend did loudly laugh and roar,
But alas! they all perished but Tom Riggles and Bill Bowls,
And they were cast on a rocky islet where on the tempest
    howls

And they lived on shell fish while they were there,
Until one day they began to despair,
But thank God they espied a vessel near at hand,
And they were taken on board and landed safe in fair
    England.

THE BATTLE OF THE ALMA, FOUGHT IN 1854

'Twas on the heights of Alma the battle began,
But the Russians turned and fled every man;
Because Sir Colin Campbell's Highland Brigade put them to
    flight,
At the charge of the bayonet, which soon ended the fight.

Sir Colin Campbell he did loudly cry,
Let the Highlanders go forward, they will win or die,
We'll hae nane but Hieland bonnets here,
So forward, my lads, and give one ringing cheer.

Then boldly and quickly they crossed the river,
But not one amongst them with fear did shiver,
And ascended the height, forming quietly on the crest,
While each man seemed anxious to do his best.

The battle was fought by twenty against one,
But the gallant British troops resolved to die to a man,
While the shot was mowing them down and making ugly
    gaps,
And shells shrieking and whistling and making fearful
    cracks.

On the heights of Alma it was a critical time,
And to see the Highland Brigade it was really sublime,
To hear the officers shouting to their men,
On lads, I'll show you the way to fight them.

Close up! Close up! Stand firm, my boys,
Now be steady, men, steady and think of our joys;
If we only conquer the Russians this day,
Our fame will be handed down to posterity for ever and aye.

Still forward! Forward! my lads was the cry,
And from the redoubt make them fly;
And at length the Russians had to give way,
And fled from the redoubt in wild dismay.

Still the fate of the battle hung in the balance,
But Sir Colin knew he had still a chance,
But one weak officer in fear loudly shouted,
Let the Guards fall back, or they'll be totally routed.

Then Sir Colin Campbell did make reply,
'Tis better, Sir, that every man of the Guards should die,
And to be found dead on this bloody field,
Than to have it said they fled and were forced to yield.

Then the Coldstreams on the Highlanders' right
Now advanced to engage the enemy in the fight,
But then they halted, unable to go forward,
Because the Russians did their progress retard.

But now came the turning point of the battle,
While the Russian guns loudly did rattle;
Then Sir Colin turned to the plumed Highland array,
And in stirring tones to them did say—

Be steady, keep silence, my lads, don't be afraid,
And make me proud of my Highland Brigade;
Then followed the command, sharp and clear,
While the war notes of the 42d bagpipes smote the ear.

The soldiers, though young, were cool and steady,
And to face the enemy they were ever ready,
And still as the bare-kneed line unwavering came on
It caused the Russians to shake and look woebegone.

And now as the din of the fight grew greater,
Fear filled the hearts of the Russian giants in stature,
Because the kilted heroes they fought so well
That they thought they had come from the regions of hell.

Oh! it was a most beautiful and magnificent display
To see the Highland Brigade in their tartan array,
And their tall bending plumes in a long line,
The scene was inspiring and really sublime.

Then, terror-stricken by this terrible advancing line,
The Russians broke down and began to whine,
And they turned round and fled with a moaning cry,
Because they were undone and had to fly.

Then the crisis was past and the victory won,
Which caused Sir Colin Campbell to cry, Well done,
And, raising his hand, gave the signal to cheer,
Which was responded to by hurrahs, loud and clear.

BEAUTIFUL ROTHESAY

Beautiful Rothesay, your scenery is most grand,
You cannot be surpassed in fair Scotland.
Tis healthy for holiday makers, to go there,
For the benefit of their health, by inhaling the pure air

And to hear the innocent birds, on a fine Summer day,
Carolling their sweet songs, so lively and gay,
Therefore, holiday makers, be advised by me,
And visit beautiful Rothesay, by the side of the Sea.

Then Sweet Jessie, let us go,
To Scotlands garden of Eden O!
And spend the lovely Summer day,
In the beautiful village of Rothesay.

There you can see the ships, passing to and fro,
Which will drive away dull care, and woe,
And, the heavens breath smells wooingly there,
Therefore, lets away dear Jessie, to inhale the balmy air.

The mansions, there, are most beautiful to be seen,
Likewise the trees, and shrubberies, green.
Therefore, we will feel happy and gay,
Walking hand in hand, together the live long day.

Along the beautiful walks with our hearts fu' cheerie,
My dear love! until we grow weary.
Then, return home at night, with our spirits light and gay,
After viewing the beautiful scenery of Rothesay.

THE BATTLE OF INKERMANN

'Twas in the year of 1854, and on the 5th of November,
When Britain will no doubt long remember,
When the Russians plotted to drive the British army into
  the sea,
But at the bayonet charge the British soon made them flee

With fourteen hundred British, fifteen thousand Russians
  were driven back,
At half-past seven o'clock in the morning they made the
  attack,
But the Grenadiers and Scottish Fusilier Guards, seven
  hundred strong,
Moved rapidly and fearlessly all along.

And their rifles were levelled ready for a volley,
But the damp had silenced their fire which made the men
    feel melancholy,
But the Russians were hurled down the ravine in a
    disordered mass
At the charge of the bayonet — an inspiring sight! — nothing
    could it surpass.

General Cathcart thought he could strike a blow at an
    unbroken Russian line;
Oh! the scene was really very sublime,
Because hand to hand they fought with a free will,
And with one magnificent charge they hurled the Russians
    down the hill.

But while General Cathcart without any dread
Was collecting his scattered forces, he fell dead,
Pierced to the heart with a Russian ball,
And his men lamented sorely his downfall.

While the Duke of Cambridge with the colours of two
    Regiments of Guards
Presses forward, and no obstacle his courage retards,
And with him about one hundred men,
And to keep up their courage he was singing a hymn to them.

Then hand to hand they fought the Russians heroically,
Which was a most inspiring sight to see;
Captain Burnaby with thirteen Guardsmen fighting
    manfully,
And they drove the Russians down the hillside right
    speedily.

The French and Zouaves aided the British in the fight,
And they shot down and killed the Russians left and right,
And the Chasseurs also joined in the fight,
And the Russians fell back in great afright.

Then the Russians tried again and again
To drive the British from the slopes of Inkermann, but all in
    vain,
For the French and British beat them back without dismay,
Until at last the Russians had to give way.

And the French and British fought side by side
Until the Russians no longer the bayonet charge could abide,
And the Russians were literally scorched by the musketry
    fire,
And in a short time the Russians were forced to retire.

Then the British and French pursued them into the depths
    of the ravine,
Oh! it was a grand sight — the scene was really sublime—
And at half-past one o'clock the Russians were defeated,
And from the field of Inkermann they sullenly retreated.

Then the Battle of Inkermann was won,
And from the field the Russians were forced to run,
But the loss of the British was terrible to behold;
The dead lay in heaps stiff and cold,
While thousands of Russians were dying with no one to aid
    them,
Alas! pitiful to relate, thousands of innocent men.

LITTLE PIERRE'S SONG

In a humble room in London sat a pretty little boy,
By the bedside of his sick mother her only joy,
Who was called Little Pierre, and who's father was dead;
There he sat poor boy, hungry and crying for bread.

There he sat humming a little song, which was his own,
But to the world it was entirely unknown,
And as he sang the song he felt heartsick,
But he resolved to get Madame Malibran to sing his song in
    public

Then he paused for a moment and clasped his hands,
And running to the looking-glass before it he stands,
Then he smoothed his yellow curls without delay,
And from a tin box takes a scroll of paper worn and grey.

Then he gave one fond eager glance at his mother,
Trying hard brave boy his grief to smother,
As he gazed on the bed where she lay,
But he resolved to see Madame Malibran without delay.

Then he kissed his mother while she slept.
And stealthly from the house he crept,
And direct to madame Malibran's house he goes,
Resolved to see her no matter who did him oppose.

And when he reached the door he knocked like a brave
    gallant
And the door was answered by her lady servant,
Then he told the servant Madame Malibran he wished to see
And the servant said, oh yes, I'll tell her immediately.

Then away the servant goes feeling quite confident,
And told her a little boy wished to see her just one moment
Oh! well, said Madame Malibran, with a smile,
Fetch in the little boy he will divert me a while.

So Little Pierre was brought in with his hat under his arm
And in his hand a scroll of paper, thinking it no harm,
Then walked straight up to Madame Malibran without dread
And said, dear lady my mother is sick and in want of bread.

And I have called to see if you would sing my little song,
At some of your grand concerts, Ah! say before long,
Or perhaps you could sell it to a publisher for a small sum,
Then I could buy food for my mother and with it would run.

Then Madame Malibran rose from her seat most costly and
    grand
And took the scroll of paper from Pierre's hand
And hummed his little song, to a plaintive air,
Then said, your song is soul stirring I do declare.

Dear child did you compose the words she asked Pierre,
Oh yes my dear lady just as you see,
Well my dear boy I will sing your song to-night,
And you shall have a seat near me on the right.

Then Pierre, said, Oh! Lady I cannot leave my mother,
But my dear boy, as for her you need not bother,
So dear child don't be the least cast down,
And in the meantime here is a crown.

And for your mother you can buy food and medicine,
So run away and be at the concert to-night in time
Then away he ran and bought many little necessary things
And while doing so his little song he hums and sings.

Then home to his poor sick mother he quickly ran,
And told her of his success with Madame Malibran,
Then his mother cried, Oh! Pierre, you are a very good boy,
And to hear of your success my heart is full of joy.

Dear mother, I am going to the concert hall to-night,
To hear Madame Malibran, which will my heart delight,
Oh! well said his mother, God speed you my little man,
I hope you will be delighted to hear Madame Malibran.

So to the concert hall he goes, and found a seat there,
And the lights and flashing of diamonds made him stare,
And caused a joyous smile to play upon his face,
For never had he been in so grand a place.

There the brave boy sat and Madame Malibran came at last
And with his eyes rivetted on her he stared aghast,
And to hear her sing, Oh! how he did long,
And he wondered if the lady would really sing his song.

At last the great singer commenced his little song,
And many a heart was moved and the plaudits loud and
    long
And as she sang it Pierre clapped his hands for joy.
That he felt as it were free from the world's annoy.

When the concert was over his heart felt as light as the air
And as for money now he didn't seem to care,
Since the great singer in Europe had sung his little song,
But he hoped that dame fortune would smile on him ere
    long

The next day he was frightened by a visit from Madame
    Malibran
And turning to his mother, she said your little boy Madame
Will make a fortune for himself and you before long,
Because I've been offered a large sum for his little song.

And Madame thank God you have such a gifted son,
But dear Madame heavens will must be done,
Then Pierre knelt and prayed that God would the lady bless
For helping them in the time of their distress.

And the memory of Pierre's prayer made the singer do more
    good
By visiting the poor and giving them clothing and food
And Pierre lightened her last moments ere her soul fled away
And he came to be one of the most talented composers of the
    day.

THE CAPTURE OF LUCKNOW

'Twas near the Begum Kothie the battle began,
Where innocent blood as plentiful as water ran;
The Begum Kothie was a place of honour given to the 93rd,
Which heroically to a man they soon did begird.

And the 4th Punjaub Rifles were their companions in glory,
And are worthy of their names enrolled in story,
Because they performed prodigious wonders in the fight,
By killing and scattering the Sepoys left and right.

The 93rd Highlanders bivouacked in a garden surrounded
    by mud walls,
Determined to capture the Begum Kothie no matter what
    befalls—
A place strongly fortified and of enormous strength,
And protected by strong earthworks of very great length.

And added to these obstacles was the most formidable of
    all–
A broad deep ditch that ran along the wall,
Which the storming party not even guessed at before;
But this barrier the British soon did climb o'er.

But early the next morning two batteries of Artillery were
    pounding away,
And the fight went on for the whole day;
And the defenders of the building kept up rattling musketry
    fire,
And when night fell the British had to retire.

Next day the contest was renewed with better success,
And the 93rd in all their beauty forward did press,
And moved on toward the position without firing a shot,
And under cover of some ruined buildings they instantly got.

And here for a few minutes they kept themselves under
    cover,
While each man felt more anxious than another
To attack the merciless rebels while it was day,
Because their blood was up and eager for the fray.

Still the enemy kept up a blazing fire at them pell-mell,
But they fired too high and not a man of them fell;
And the bullets whistled around them again and again,
Still on went the unwavering Highlanders with might and
    main.

But when they reached the ditch they were taken by
    surprise,
By the unexpected obstacle right before their eyes;
But Captain Middleton leapt into the ditch and showed
    them the way,
And immediately the whole of the men were after him
    without delay.

Leith Hay himself was among the first across,
And gained a footing on the other side without any personal
    loss;
And he assisted in helping the rest out of the ditch,
While the din of war was at the highest pitch.

'Twas then the struggle commenced in terrible earnest:
While every man was resolved to do his best;
And the enemy barricaded every entrance so as a single man
    could only pass,
Determined to make a strong resistance, and the British to
    harass.

But barrier after barrier soon was passed;
And the brave men no doubt felt a little harassed,
But they fought desperately and overturned their foes at
  every point,
And put the rebels to flight by shot and bayonet conjoint.

The Sheiks and the Horse Guards behaved right well—
Because beneath their swords, by the score, the Sepoys fell;
And their beautiful war steeds did loudly neigh and roar,
While beneath their hoofs they trampled them all o'er.

And as for John McLeod — the pipe-major of the 93rd,
He kept sounding his bagpipes and couldn't be stirred—
Because he remembered his duty in the turmoil,
And in the battlefield he was never known to recoil.

And as for Major General McBain — he was the hero in the
  fight;
He fought heroically — like a lion — with all his might;
And again and again he was met by desperate odds,
But he scattered them around him and made them kiss the
  sods.

And he killed eleven of the enemy with sword in hand,
Which secured for him the proudest of all honours in the
  land,
Namely, that coveted honour called the Victoria Cross,
Of which many a deserving hero has known the loss.

And as for brave Hodson — he was a warrior born,
And military uniform did his body adorn;
And his voice could be heard in the battle afar,
Crying — "Come on my boys there is nothing like war!

But, in a moment, a volley was discharged at him,
And he fell mortally wounded, while the Sepoys did grin;
Then the Highlanders closed with their foes and made them
    retreat,
And left them not till every rebel lay dead at their feet.

Then Sir Colin Campbell to his men did say, —
"Men, I feel proud that we have captured Lucknow this
    day;
Therefore strike up the bagpipes and give one hearty cheer,
And enjoy yourselves, my heroes, while ye are here."

THE BURNS STATUE

This Statue, I must confess, is magnificent to see,
And I hope will long be appreciated by the people of Dundee;
It has been beautifully made by Sir John Steell,
And I hope the pangs of hunger he will never feel.

This Statue is most elegant in its design,
And I hope will defy all weathers for a very long time;
And I hope strangers from afar with admiration will stare
On this beautiful statue of thee, Immortal Bard of Ayr.

Fellow-citizens, this Statue seems most beautiful to the eye,
Which would cause Kings and Queens for such a one to sigh,
And make them feel envious while passing by
In fear of not getting such a beautiful Statue after they die.

THE HERO OF KALAPORE: AN INCIDENT
OF THE INDIAN MUTINY

The 27th Regiment has mutinied at Kalapore:
That was the substance of a telegram, which caused a great
    uproar
At Sattara, on the evening of the 8th of July,
And when the British officers heard it, they heaved a bitter
    sigh.

'Twas in the year of 1857,
Which will long be remembered: Oh! Heaven!
That the Sepoys revolted, and killed their British officers
    and their wives;
Besides, they killed their innocent children, not sparing one
    of their lives.

There was one man there who was void of fear,
He was the brave Lieutenant William Alexander Kerr;
And to face the rebels boldly it was his intent,
And he assured his brother officers his men were true to the
    Government.

And now that the danger was so near at hand,
He was ready to put his men to the test, and them
    command;
And march to the rescue of his countrymen at Kalapore,
And try to quell the mutiny and barbarous uproar.

And in half an hour he was ready to start,
With fifty brave horsemen, fearless and smart;
And undaunted Kerr and his horsemen rode on without
    dismay,
And in the middle of the rainy season, which was no child's
    play.

And after a toilsome march they reached Kalapore,
To find their countrymen pressed very hard and sore;
The mutineers had attacked and defeated the Kalapore
    Light Infantry,
Therefore their fellow countrymen were in dire extremity.

Then the Sepoys established themselves in a small square
    fort;
It was a place of strength, and there they did resort;
And Kerr had no guns to batter down the gate,
But nevertheless he felt undaunted, and resigned to his
    fate.

And darkness was coming on and no time was to be lost,
And he must attack the rebels whatever be the cost;
Therefore he ordered his troopers to prepare to storm the
    fort,
And at the word of command towards it they did resort.

And seventeen troopers advanced to the attack,
And one of his men, Gumpunt Row Deo Kerr, whose
    courage wasn't slack;
So great was his courage he couldn't be kept back,
So he resolved with Lieutenant Kerr to make the attack.

Then with crowbars they dashed at the doors vigorously,
Whilst bullets rained around them, but harmlessly;
So they battered on the doors until one gave way,
Then Lieutenant Kerr and his henchmen entered without
    dismay.

Then Kerr's men rushed in sword in hand,
Oh! what a fearful onslaught, the mutineers couldn't it
  withstand,
And Kerr's men with straw set the place on fire,
And at last the rebels were forced to retire.

And took refuge in another house, and barricaded it fast,
And prepared to defend themsleves to the last;
Then Lieutenant Kerr and Row Deo Kerr plied the
  crowbars again,
And heavy blows on the woodwork they did rain.

Then the door gave way and they crawled in,
And they two great heroes side by side did begin
To charge the mutineers with sword in hand, which made
  them grin,
Whilst the clashing of swords and bayonets made a fearful
  din.

Then hand to hand, and foot to foot, a fierce combat
  began,
Whilst the blood of the rebels copiously ran,
And a ball cut the chain of Kerr's helmet in two,
And another struck his sword, but the man he slew.

Then a Sepoy clubbed his musket and hit Kerr on the
  head,
But fortunately the blow didn't kill him dead;
He only staggered, and was about to be bayoneted by a
  mutineer,
But Gumpunt Kerr laid his assailant dead without fear.

Kerr's little party were now reduced to seven,
Yet fearless and undaunted, and with the help of Heaven,
He gathered his small band possessed of courage bold,
Determined to make a last effort to capture the stronghold.

Then he cried, "My men, we will burn them out,
And suffocate them with smoke, without any doubt!"
So bundles of straw and hay were found without delay,
And they set fire to them against the doors without dismay.

Then Kerr patiently waited till the doors were consumed,
And with a gallant charge, the last attack was resumed,
And he dashed sword in hand into the midst of the
    mutineers,
And he and his seven troopers played great havoc with their
    sabres.

So by the skillful war tactics of brave Lieutenant Kerr,
He defeated the Sepoy mutineers and rescued his country.
    men dear;
And but for Lieutenant Kerr the British would have met
    with a great loss,
And for his great service he received the Victoria Cross.

JACK HONEST, OR THE WIDOW AND HER SON

Jack Honest was only eight years of age when his father
    died,
And by the death of his father, Mrs Honest was sorely
    tried;
And Jack was his father's only joy and pride,
And for honesty Jack couldn't be equallyed in the
    country-side.

So a short time before Jack's father died,
'Twas loud and bitterly for Jack he cried,
And bade him sit down by his bedside,
And then told him to be honest whatever did betide.

John, he said, looking him earnestly in the face,
Never let your actions your name disgrace,
Remember, my dear boy, and do what's right,
And God will bless you by day and night.

Then Mr Honest bade his son farewell, and breathed his
   last,
While the hot tears from Jack's eyes fell thick and fast;
And the poor child did loudly sob and moan,
When he knew his father had left him and his mother
   alone.

So, as time wore on, Jack grew to be a fine boy,
And was to his mother a help and a joy;
And, one evening, she said, Jack, you are my only prop,
I must tell you, dear, I'm thinking about opening a shop.

Oh! that's a capital thought, mother, cried Jack,
And to take care of the shop I won't be slack;
Then his mother said, Jackey, we will try this plan,
And look to God for his blessing, and do all we can.

So the widow opened the shop and succeeded very well,
But in a few months fresh troubles her befell —
Alas! poor Mrs Honest was of fever taken ill,
But Jack attended his mother with a kindly will.

But, for fear of catching the fever, her customers kept
   away,
And once more there wasn't enough money the rent to
   pay;
And in her difficulties Mrs Honest could form no plan to
   get out,
But God would help her, she had no doubt.

So, one afternoon, Mrs Honest sent Jack away
To a person that owed her some money, and told him not
   to stay,
But when he got there the person had fled,
And to return home without the money he was in
   dread.

So he saw a gentleman in a carriage driving along at a
   rapid rate,
And Jack ran forward to his mansion and opened the
   lodge-gate,
Then the gentleman opened his purse and gave him, as he
   thought, a shilling
For opening the lodge-gate so cleverly and so willing.

Then Jack stooped to lift up the coin, when, lo and
   behold!
He found to his surprise it was a piece of gold!
And Jack cried oh! joyful, this will make up my mother's
   loss,
Then he ran home speedily, knowing his mother wouldn't
   be cross.

And when he got home he told his mother of his ill
    success,
And his adventure with the gentleman, then she felt deep
    distress;
And when Jack showed her the sovereign, the gentleman
    gave him,
She cried, We mustn't keep that money, it would be a sin.

Dear mother, I thought so, there must be some mistake,
But in the morning, to Squire Brooksby, the sovereign
    I'll take;
So, when morning came, he went to Squire Brooksby's
    Hall,
And at the front door for the Squire he loudly did call.

Then the hall door was opened by a footman, dressed in
    rich livery,
And Jack told him he wished Mr Brooksby to see;
Then to deliver Jack's message the footman withdrew,
And when the footman returned he said, Master will see you.

Then Jack was conducted into a rich furnished room,
And to Mr Brooksby he told his errand very soon,
While his honest heart, with fear, didn't quake,
Saying, Mr Brooksby, you gave me a sovereign yesterday
    in a mistake.

Why, surely I have seen you before, said Mr Brooksby;
Yes, Sir, replied Jack Honest, bowing very politely;
Then what is your name, my honest lad? asked Mr
    Brooksby;
John Honest, sir, replied Jack, right fearlessly.

Then, my brave lad, you are Honest by name, and honest
   by nature,
Which, really, you appear to be in every feature,
But, I am afraid, such boys as you are very few,
But, I dare say, your mother has taught you.

Then Jack laid the sovereign down on the table before
   Mr Brooksby;
But Mr Brooksby said, No! my lad, I freely give it to thee;
Then Jack said, Oh, sir, I'm obliged to you I'm sure,
Because, sir, this money will help my mother, for she is
   poor.

Mrs Brooksby came to see Mrs Honest in a few days,
And for Jack's honesty she was loud in praise;
And she took Jack into her service, and paid him liberally,
And she gave Mrs Honest a house, for life, rent free.

Now, I must leave Jack Honest and his mother in fresh-
   found glory,
Hoping my readers will feel interested in this story,
And try always to imitate the hero — Jack Honest —
And I'm sure they will find it the safest and the best!

THE DOWNFALL OF DELHI

'Twas in the year of 1857 and on the 14th of September
That the Sepoy rebels at Delhi were forced to surrender;
The attack was first to be made by Brigadier Nicholson,
And he was ordered to attack the Cashmere Bastion.

The British were entirely in command
Of Major-General Reid, assisted by Brigadier-Generals
    Wilson and Burnand;
After a long march, fighting through a hostile country,
And the brave heroes took up a position before the city.

Delhi gates were encircled with a fringe of fire,
But the British resolved to die rather than retire;
And the brave fellows rushed towards the gate
Carrying the powder bags that were to seal the Sepoys'
    fate.

Here their progress was checked, for the drawbridge was
    destroyed,
But the British felt very little annoyed,
Because a few planks were across the chasm thrown,
Then a match was applied to the powder bags, and into
    atoms the gate was blown.

Then the rebel artillerymen with terror fled,
For the streets were strewn by the Sepoy dead;
Then the British charged them without fear,
Shouting "On boys, on, for our Queen and Country dear."

Then Lieutenant Home gave orders to advance,
And charge them with your bayonets, it is our only
    chance;
And with a ringing British cheer they charged them
    fearlessly,
And they drove the enemy before them through the
    streets of the city.

Then the young bugler blew a blast loud and clear,
Which was answered by a British ringing cheer;
But General Nicholson was killed, which was a great loss,
And afterwards the bugler was decorated with the Victoria
    Cross.

General Jones formed a junction with Colonel Campbell's
    Regiment,
And to enter by the Cashmere Gate they were bent;
And they advanced through the streets without delay,
And swept all before them through the gate without
    dismay.

The streets were filled with mutineers who fought
    savagely,
Determined to fight to the last and die heroically,
While the alarm drums did beat, and the cannons did roar,
And the dead and the dying lay weltering in their gore.

And the rebels fought for King Timour like tigers in a cage,
He was a very old man, more than ninety years of age;
And their shouts and yells were fearful to hear,
While the shrill sound of the bugle smote on the ear.

The British dash at Delhi will never be forgot,
For the chief instigators of the mutiny were shot;
And their bodies in the Mayor's court were hung,
And as the people gazed thereon, their hearts with anguish
    were wrung.

And that evening General Wilson drank the health of the
   Queen,
Also his officers hailed her Empress of India, which
   enhanced the scene;
While the assembled thousands shouted "God save the
   Queen!"
Oh! it was a most beautiful scene.

Delhi was glorious prize, for the city was full of jewels
   and gold,
Besides a hundred pieces of cannon, be it told;
But dearly was the victory gained,
But in the book of fame the British are famed.:
Oh, it was a glorious and heroic victory,
And will be handed down to posterity.

THE RIVER OF LEITH

As I stood upon the Dean Bridge and viewed the beautiful
   scenery,
I felt fascinated and my heart was full of glee,
And I exclaimed in an ecstasy of delight,
In all my travels I never saw such a sight.

The scenery is so enchanting to look upon
That all tourists will say, "Dull care, be gone."
'Tis certainly a most lovely spot,
And once seen it can never be forgot.

Then away! away! to the River of Leith,
That springs from the land of heather and heath,
And view the gorgeous scenery on a fine summer day.
I'm sure it will drive dull care away.

The water-fall near the Bridge is most beautiful to be
    seen,
As it falls and shines like crystal in the sunsheen;
And the sound can be heard all day long,
While the innocent trouts sing an aquatic song.

The glen is a cool spot in the summer time.
There the people can be shaded from the sunshine
Under the spreading branches of the big trees,
And there's seats there to rest on if they please.

Then near St Bernard's Well there's a shady bower,
Where the lovers, if they like, can spend an hour;
And while they rest there at their ease
They can make love to each other if they please.

The water of St Bernard's Well is very nice,
But to get a drink of it one penny is the price.
I think in justice the price is rather high,
To give a penny for a drink when one feels dry.

The braes of the River Leith is most charming to be seen,
With its beautiful trees and shrubberies green,
And as the tourist gazes on the river in the valley below,
His heart with joy feels all aglow.

There the little trouts do sport and play
During the live-long summer day,
While the bee and butterfly is on the wing,
And with the singing of birds the glen doth ring.

The walk underneath the Dean Bridge is lovely to see.
And as ye view the scenery it will fill your heart with glee.
It is good for the people's health to be walking there
As they gaze on the beauties of Nature and inhale pure
    air.

The Dean Bridge is a very magnificent sight,
Because from the basement it is a great height.
And it seems most attractive to the eye,
And arrests the attention of strangers as they pass by.

The braes of Belgrave Crescent is lovely to see,
With its beautiful walks and green shrubbery.
'Tis health for the people that lives near by there
To walk along the bonny walks and breathe the sweet air.

Therefore all lovers of the picturesque, be advised by me
And the beautiful scenery of the River Leith go and see,
And I am sure you will get a very great treat,
Because the River of Leith scenery cannot be beat.

THE ASHANTEE WAR: THE FALL OF COOMASSIE

'Twas in the year of 1874, and on New Year's Day,
The British Army landed at Elmina without dismay,
And numbering in all, 1400 bayonets strong,
And all along the Cape Coast they fearlessly marched
    along,
Under the command of Sir Garnet Wolseley, a hero bold,
And an honour to his King and country, be it told.

And between them and Coomassie, lay a wilderness of
    jungle,
But they marched on boldly without making a stumble,
And under a tropical sun, upwards of an hundred miles,
While their bayonets shone bright as they marched on in
    files.

Coomassie had to be reached and King Coffee's power
    destroyed,
And, before that was done the British were greatly
    annoyed,
Lieutenant Lord Gifford, with his men gained the Crest of
    the Adenisi Hills,
And when they gained the top, with joy their hearts fills.

Sir John McLeod was appointed General of the Black
    Brigade,
And a great slaughter of the enemy they made,
And took possession of an Ashantee village,
And fought like lions in a fearful rage.

While the British troops most firmly stood,
And advanced against a savage horde concealed in a wood,
Yet the men never flinched, but entered the wood fearlessly,
And all at once the silence was broken by a roar of musketry.

And now the fight began in real earnest,
And the Black Watch men resolved to do their best,
While the enemy were ambushed in the midst of the wood,
Yet the Highlanders their ground firmly stood.

And the roar of the musketry spread through the jungle,
Still the men crept on without making a stumble,
And many of the Black Watch fell wounded and dead,
And Major Macpherson was wounded, but he rallied his
   men without dread.

The battle raged for five hours, but the Highlanders were
   gaining ground,
Until the bagpipes struck up their wild clarion sound,
Then the dusky warriors fled in amazement profound,
Because their comrades were falling on every side around.

Sir Archibald Alison led on the Highland Brigade,
And great havoc amongst the enemy they made,
And village after village they captured and destroyed,
Until King Coffee lost heart and felt greatly annoyed.

Sir John McLeod took the command of his own regiment,
And with a swinging pace into the jaws of death they
   went,
Fearlessly firing by companies in rotation,
And dashed into a double Zone of Fire without hesitation.

And in that manner the Black Watch pressed onward,
And the enemy were powerless their progress to retard,
Because their glittering bayonets were brought into play,
And panic stricken the savage warriors fled in great dismay.

Then Sir Garnet Wolseley with his men entered Coomassie
   at night,
Supported by half the rifles and Highlanders — a most
   beautiful sight,
And King Coffee and his army had fled,
And thousands of his men on the field were left dead.

And King Coffee, he was crushed at last,
And the poor King felt very downcast,
And his sorrow was really profound,
When he heard that Coomassie was burned to the ground.

Then the British embarked for England without delay,
And with joy their hearts felt gay,
And by the end of March they reached England,
And the reception they received was very grand.

THE BEAUTIFUL CITY OF PERTH

Beautiful and ancient city of Perth,
One of the grandest upon the earth,
With your stately mansions and streets so clean,
And situated betwixt two Inches green,
Which are most magnificent to be seen.

The North Inch is beautiful to behold,
Where the daisies and butter-cups their petals unfold,
In the warm summer time of the year,
While the clear silvery Tay rolls by quite near,
And such a scene will your spirits cheer.

The South Inch is lovely, be it said,
And a splendid spot for military parade,
While along the highway there are some big trees,
Where the soldiers can rest or stand at ease,
Whichever way their commanders please.

The surrounding woodland scenery is very grand,
It cannot be surpassed in fair Scotland,
Especially the elegant Palace of Scone, in history renowned,
Where some of Scotland's kings were crowned.

And the Fair Maid of Perth's house is worthy to be seen,
Which is well worth visiting by Duke, Lord, or Queen;
The Fair Maid of Perth caused the battle on the North Inch
'Twixt the Clans Chattan and Kay, and neither of them did
    flinch,
Until they were cut up inch by inch.

The scenery is lovely in the month of June,
When trees and flowers are in full bloom,
Especially near by the Palace of Scone,
Where the blackbird is heard whistling all day
While near by rolls on the clear silvery Tay.

Of all the cities in Scotland, beautiful Perth for me,
For it is the most elegant city that ever I did see,
With its beautiful woodland scenery along the river Tay,
Which would make the tourist's heart feel gay,
While fishing for trout on a fine summer day.

There, the angler, if he likes to resort
For a few day's fishing, can have excellent sport,
And while he is fishing during the day,
He will feel delighted with the scenery along the river Tay.
And the fish he catches will drive dull care away,
And his toil will be rewarded for the fatigues of the day.

Beautiful city of Perth, magnificent to be seen,
With your grand statues and Inches green,
And your lovely maidens fair and gay,
Which, in conclusion, I will venture to say,
You cannot be surpassed at the present day.

GENERAL ROBERTS IN AFGHANISTAN

'Twas in the year of 1878, and the winter had set in,
Lord Roberts and the British Army their march did begin,
On their way to Afghanistan to a place called Cabul;
And the weather was bitter cold and the rivers swollen and
    full.

And the enemy were posted high up amongst the hills,
And when they saw the British, with fear their blood thrills;
The savages were camped on the hillsides in war array,
And occupying a strong position which before the British
    lay.

And viewed from the front their position was impregnable,
But Lord Roberts was a general of great skill;
Therefore to surprise the enemy he thought it was right,
To march upon the enemy in the dead of night.

Then the men were mustered without delay,
And each man of them was eager for the fray;
And in the silent darkness they felt no dismay,
And to attack the enemy they marched boldly away.

And on they marched bravely without fear or doubt,
And about daybreak the challenge of an Afghan sentinel
    rang out,
And echoed from rock to rock on the frosty biting air;
But the challenge didn't the British scare.

Then the Highlanders attacked them left and right,
And oh! it was a gorgeous and an inspiring sight;
For a fierce hand to hand struggle raged for a time,
While the pibrochs skirled aloud, oh! the scene was
    sublime.

Then the Ghoorkas did the Afghans fiercely attack,
And at every point and turning they were driven back;
And a fierce hand to hand struggle raged for a time,
While in the morning sunshine the British bayonets did
    shine.

And around the ridge or knoll the battle raged for three
    hours,
And British bullets fell amongst them in showers;
For Captain Kelso brought us his mountain battery,
And sent his shells right into the camp of the enemy,
Then the left of the Afghans was turned, and began to flee.

Meanwhile, on the enemy's strong position Lord Roberts
    launched an attack,
And from their position they could hardly be driven back
Because the Afghans were hid amongst the woods and hills,
Still with undaunted courage, the British blood thrills.

And the Afghans pressed the British hotly, but they didn't
    give way,
For the 8th Ghoorkas and the 72nd kept them at bay;
And the mountain guns shells upon them did fire,
Then the 8th Punjaub, bounding up the heights, made
    them retire.

Then Major White seized a rifle from one of his men and
    did retire,
And levelled the piece fearlessly and did fire;
And with a steady and well-timed shot
He shot the Afghan leader dead on the spot.

Then the British with a wild cheer dashed at them,
And on each side around they did them hem;
And at the bayonet charge they drove them down the hill,
And in hundreds they did them kill.

Then in a confused mass they fled down the opposite side
    of the hill
In hundreds, driven by sheer force sore against their will;
And helter-skelter they did run,
For all their positions were carried and the victory won.

Then on the 8th of August again Lord Roberts' march
    began
For to fight the rebel Ayoob Khan;
And with an army about seven thousand strong
On his way to Candahar he fearlessly marched along.

And the battle that followed at Candahar was a complete
    victory,
And Lord Roberts' march to Candahar stands unrivalled
    in history;
And let's thank God that sent Lord Roberts to conquer
    Ayoob Khan,
For from that time there's been no more war in
    Afghanistan.

Success to Lord Roberts; he's a very brave man,
For he conquered the Afghans in Afghanistan,
With an army about seven thousand strong,
He spread death and desolation all along.

REQUISITION TO THE QUEEN

1. Most August! Empress of India, and of great Britain the
      Queen,
   I most humbly beg your pardon, hoping you will not
      think it mean
   That a poor poet that lives in Dundee,
   Would be so presumptous to write unto Thee

2. Most lovely Empress of India, and Englands generous
      Queen,
   I send you an Address, I have written on Scotlands Bard,
   Hoping that you will accept it, and not be with me to
      hard,
   Nor fly into a rage, but be as Kind and Condescending
   As to give me your Patronage

3. Beautiful Empress, of India, and Englands Gracious
      Queen,
   I send you a Shakespearian Address written by me.
   And I think if your Majesty reads it, right pleased you
      will be.
   And my heart it will leap with joy, if it is patronized by
      Thee.

4. Most Mighty Empress, of India, and Englands beloved
      Queen,
         Most Handsome to be Seen.
         I wish you every Success.
         And that heaven may you bless.

For your Kindness to the poor while they are in distress.
I hope the Lord will protect you while living
    And hereafter when your Majesty is ... dead.
I hope Thee Lord above will place an eternal Crown!
        upon your Head.
    I am your Gracious Majesty ever faithful to Thee,
William McGonagall, The Poor Poet,
    That lives in Dundee.